Can you make a balloon-powered trolley? Or hold a glass full of water upside down without spilling a drop? Or make a paper-clip hover in the air with no visible means of support? This book will show you how to carry out these and many other exciting – but simple – experiments in your own home.

Cover illustration by Graham Round

Experiments for you

John Tollyfield

Illustrated by Ray Martin

Evans Brothers Limited London

Published by Evans Brothers Limited
Montague House, Russell Square,
London, W.C.1.

© Evans Brothers Limited 1972

First published 1972
Reprinted 1975

Set in 12 on 14 point Baskerville
Printed in Great Britain by
Cox & Wyman Ltd.,
London, Reading and Fakenham

CSD ISBN 0 237 35131 5   PRA 4304
PB ISBN 0 237 35104 8

Contents

To Hugh, recently young, with thanks
for help and technical advice.

Something to Read First

It is nice to make things, and do things, and find out about things. Just getting started is sometimes difficult. Once you have a model made, or something set up which works, ideas come to you and one thing leads to another. This book aims to give you starting ideas. Carry on and develop them; you will find it fun.

Materials to Use

Make use of odds and ends wherever possible. Here are some things which will be useful:

Empty toothpaste tubes
Ice-lolly sticks
Empty tins
Jam jars

Used-up ball-point pens
Matchboxes
Cardboard boxes

Corks
Balloons
Cardboard tubes
Cream cartons

Washing-up liquid bottles (both kinds, 'squeezy' and see-through)

You will be surprised to find how many useful things mother has in the kitchen, and your father in his tool-box or desk has a lot, too. Things like these:

Plastic milk straws	Cocktail sticks	Aluminium foil
Citric acid	Soda bicarbonate	Washing-up liquid
See-through cook- ing foil	Cotton	Typewriting paper
	Rubber bands	Paper fasteners
Paper clips	Oil	Ink
Pins	Sandpaper	Pepper
String	Coffee filter papers	Sellotape
Blotting-paper		

There are a few things you may have to buy:

Balsa Wood　You can get this in most model shops. It is very light and easy to use. Get one piece 75 mm wide, 10 mm thick and 610 mm long. This will do for a number of models. Get also three balsa wood strips, 6 mm square and 610 mm long.

Plastic flexible tube　You can get this at most of those chemist shops where they sell supplies for wine-making. You need about 2 metres. The hole down the centre of the tube should be about 6 mm across.

Magnets　You can get good magnets at most ironmongers' shops. They are made by the 'Eclipse' Company. Get a horseshoe shaped one.

Adhesive　There are many useful materials for sticking. The simplest to use is one that comes in a tube. Bostik 1 or Uhu are recommended because they stick to metal as well as wood. (Make sure always to put the pin back in the top after using the glue.)

Cardboard   You may have to buy this at a stationer's shop, but very often there is something suitable at home. Postcards are suitable for thin card. Thick card you can usually get by cutting up a shoe-box.

Nobody can make things without tools. You will need just a few simple ones:

Modelling knife   You will be able to get this where you get the balsa wood. It will be sharp, so mind your fingers and keep the guard on when it is not in use.

Small hacksaw

Scissors

Small hammer

Ruler marked in millimetres (mm)

Thinking

This is something you cannot help doing as you go along. There will be questions which you want to ask. I have tried to guess at some of the things which you might ask about, and I have put the questions in at various places. At the end of the book, on pages 83–89, I have given some answers.

Well! Now you can start work!

Water Experiments

1 Tricks with water in a glass tumbler

There once lived a man called Hero of Alexandria. His time was around the year 150 B.C. He wrote a book in Greek which we would find difficult to read. Fortunately it has been translated into English. This is one of the things which he says in his book:

'Let a vessel which seems to be empty be inverted, and, being carefully kept upright, pressed down into water; the water will not enter it even though it be completely immersed.'

Would you like to try Hero's experiment? You can do it if you like as a kind of trick for your friends. You say to them: 'Can you put a handkerchief under water without getting it wet?' They may know the way, but if not you can show them. Suppose we call this one:

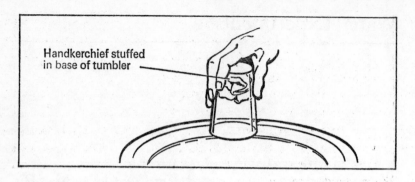

Handkerchief stuffed in base of tumbler

Hero's Handkerchief Experiment

1 Take a dry glass tumbler and stuff the handkerchief into the bottom of it as shown in the picture, so that you can turn the glass upsidedown without the handkerchief falling out.

2 Now, with the glass still upsidedown, slowly push it into water in the sink or washing-up bowl. You will find that water rises up inside the glass, but does not get high enough to touch the handkerchief; not even if you push the glass right down underneath the water.

Do you think that Hero surprised his own friends like this? In his book he is able to say *why* it happens. Can you?

There is another experiment with water in a tumbler which I like doing. If it goes wrong though, it can be a bit messy. Make sure you do this one close to the sink. We can call it:

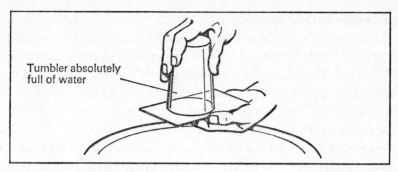

Tumbler absolutely full of water

Water that does not fall

1 Take your glass tumbler and fill it absolutely full of water. It needs to be right up to the brim, and standing up above the brim in the way that water does.

2 Then you need a postcard or any piece of fairly stiff card which is larger than the top of the tumbler. Slide this piece of card gently across the tumbler's mouth. It should seal it up so that there is no air underneath.

3 Now comes the tricky bit! Put one hand flat against the card so as to press it against the mouth of the tumbler. Turn the tumbler upsidedown, keeping your hand in position. Then take your hand away. Does all the water run out, pushing the card away? If you hold it quite level so that there is no slipping of the card, it will stay there. Why? There is not any sticky stuff there, is there?

But, be careful with this one. If you let your hand slip a bit, the card can slide to one side, and then there will be a horrible splash. So hold it over the sink. It is perfectly safe if you have a steady hand.

2 A can full of magic

Following our experiments with water in a glass, how would you like to make a can from which water will run when you tell it to? Then it will stop when you tell it to stop. At least, your friends may *think* that the can is obeying the words you speak to it. There is a trick in it, of course. You can let them into the secret afterwards.

The Magic Can

1 The best kind of can for this is an empty syrup tin. It usually has a lid which fits inside the rim and can be pushed in tight.

2 You need to make two holes in the can; one in the centre of the bottom, the other in the centre of the lid. You can do each of these most easily by holding a two-inch nail (or one about that size) with its point just where you want the hole. Then give it a good hard tap with a hammer. (In each case, tap the nail from outside the can inwards: this leaves a smooth finish on the outside.)

3 With the lid off, holding one finger against the hole in the bottom, let the can fill up with water from the tap. Put the can down in the sink and press the lid on. It does not matter if some water runs out of the bottom hole while you are doing this.

4 To get some practice, hold the can up in one hand with one finger over the hole in the lid. If all is well you will find that the water does not run out of the hole in the bottom. But, just move your finger to one side slightly so that it no

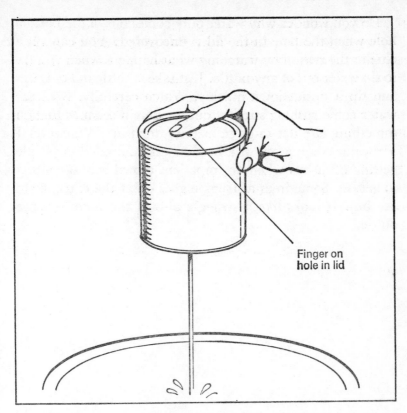

Finger on
hole in lid

longer covers up the hole in the lid completely, and the
water will stream out of the bottom hole.

5 Now for showing it as a trick! Hold it up high so that your
friends cannot see your finger over the hole in the lid. Tell
the can to 'Start' or 'Stop' and move your finger slightly
to make it obey you. (Make sure you have something
underneath to catch the water when it flows.)

Do you wonder why water only comes out of the bottom hole when the hole in the lid is uncovered? You can get a clue to the reason by watching what happens when you try to tip water out of any bottle. Just take a bottle full of water and tip it upsidedown quickly. Watch carefully. Does the water come rushing straight out, or does it seem as though something else has to go in at the same time? Whenever I see water coming out of a bottle I am reminded of people getting off a bus when an impatient crowd is also waiting to get on. Sometimes a struggle goes on at the entrance to the bus. It looks like a struggle also at the mouth of the bottle.

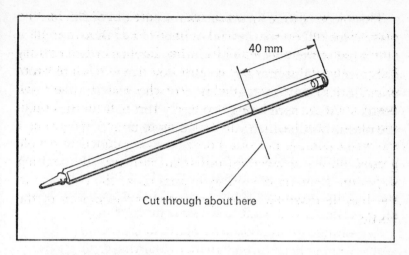

40 mm

Cut through about here

3 A diver in a bottle

Did you make the 'Magic Can' obey you? Now try making a diver who will go up and down for you. Again, it may be a surprise to other people to see how he will obey you. Let us call him:

The Obedient Diver

1 You need a piece of plastic tube about 40 mm long, closed at one end. I found that the top cut off a used-up ball-point pen was good for this. I mean, of course, the outside case which goes round the ink tube. The top of this usually has a little plastic stopper which comes out easily. This is useful when you come to put the diver in water. Cut off the top 40 mm of the ball-point pen tube carefully using your small hacksaw. (Take the ink tube out first or cut round it. It makes a mess if you happen to cut through it.)

19

2 This piece of tube forms the main part of your diver. To make it look like a man, cut the shape of a man 44 mm high out of flat white plastic. The kind you get in cream cartons does nicely. Paint him any colours you like with waterproof paint. Stick him on to the side of the plastic tube with Bostik 1. Make sure he will go easily through the mouth of the plastic bottle which you are going to use.

3 The plastic bottle needs to be the kind you can see through. Mother often gets this kind if she buys 'Palmolive' washing-up liquid, or some kinds of orange squash. Clean off the labels if you want to see your diver clearly.

The orange squash bottle will have a screw cap, probably, and a nice big neck through which your diver will go easily. Bottles for washing-up liquid have only tiny holes for the liquid to come out of. But, if you pull the top plastic part hard you will find it all comes off. This leaves an opening about 14 mm across. That should be big enough for your diver to go through.

4 Fill the bottle right up to the top with water. Stand it alongside a washing-up bowl which has water in it to a depth of about 100 mm. Try your diver in the water in the bowl. If his tube is empty, he will float. If his tube is full, he sinks. How do you get water into the tube? Take out the little plastic plug at the top. Push the diver into the water. Put the plug back in under water. Let go of the diver and he will sink. How could you make him just not float and just not sink? Have the tube *part* full, of course. So pull out the plug and let a little water in or out. Keep doing this until your

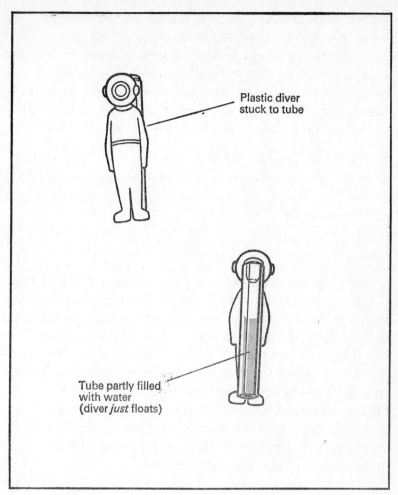

Plastic diver
stuck to tube

Tube partly filled
with water
(diver *just* floats)

diver floats, *but only just*. This is the difficult part, but keep trying.

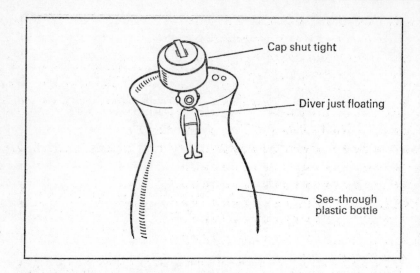

Cap shut tight

Diver just floating

See-through plastic bottle

5 Now, lift your diver carefully. Put him into the full bottle. (Do not worry, the water will stay in the tube while you do this. You probably know why.) Close the top of the bottle tightly. Then the diver should be floating just beneath the cap. How can you make him dive? What are you going to try first? Shaking the bottle? Try a number of things, and you may suddenly find out how to make him go down. It is fun if you find out for yourself. If you don't though, don't be disappointed. It tells you what to do at the back of the book, on page 83. It also tells you *why* he goes up and down, just in case you have not spotted the reason.

I hope you have fun with your diver. People have been making them on the same principle for many years. Sometimes you will hear him called 'The Cartesian Diver'.

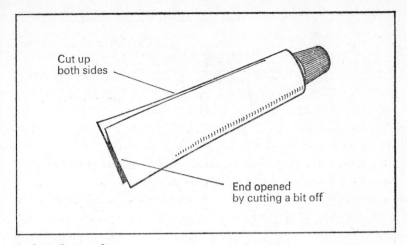

Cut up
both sides

End opened
by cutting a bit off

4 A submarine

A submarine hides at the bottom of the sea. It comes to the surface when it is time to attack. A real one has oil engines, or else runs on atomic power. Try making a model one which uses citric acid and soda bicarbonate. Your mother will know about these two things. She uses them in cooking. Ask her to let you have about a teaspoonful of each.

Now you can start. You need an empty toothpaste tube and two flat ice-lolly sticks. Let us call it:

The Lolly Stick Submarine

1 Flatten out the empty toothpaste tube. Cut off a bit at the bottom so that you can open it at that end. Slit up the sides of the tube with a pair of scissors until about 6 mm from the top to form a pair of long flaps. Clean out remains of the toothpaste in warm water. Make sure that the nozzle is clear and that the cap screws on cleanly.

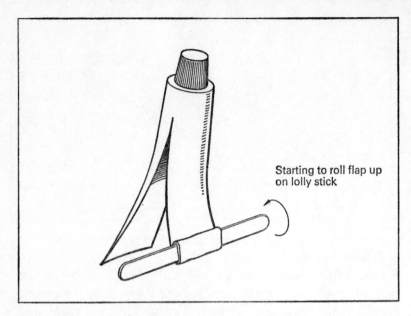

Starting to roll flap up on lolly stick

2 Start rolling one of the flaps round the middle of one lolly stick until it is close to the top. Do the same with the other flap and the other lolly stick.

3 The two lolly sticks and the two rolls of tube upon them need holding apart in the middle with two pieces of cork about 6 mm thick. Cut these from a bottle cork with your sharp knife and stick them in place with Bostik 1.

4 To form the bow and the stern of the submarine, pull the lolly sticks together at front and back. Put pins through to hold them together and stick them with Bostik 1. When the glue is dry the pins can come out.

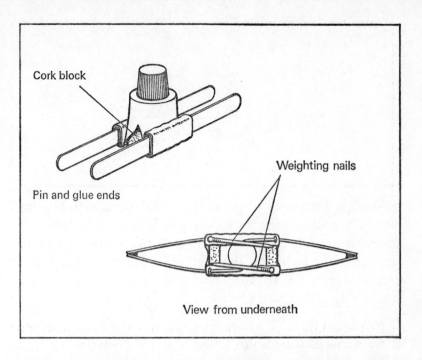

Cork block

Pin and glue ends

Weighting nails

View from underneath

5 Is your model beginning to look like a submarine? Now you need to weight it, so that on its own it just sinks in water. Make it heavier by sticking nails or pennies underneath with Bostik 1, or if it sinks too quickly stick on some pieces of cork or balsa wood to make it lighter in the water. Keep testing until you get it just right.

6 Now see if you can make it come to the surface. Make a mixture of equal parts of citric acid and soda bicarbonate. You need enough of each to cover a one new penny coin. Wrap the mixture in a little screw of tissue paper.

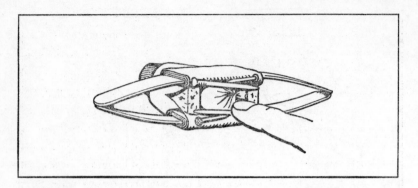

7 Wedge this screw of paper into the space between the two lolly sticks so that it comes just beneath the 'conning tower' formed by the top of the toothpaste tube. Unscrew the cap of the tube. Put the submarine into a bowl of water (or the bath). Let it fill up and sink to the bottom. Screw the cap tight on again while it is resting on the bottom.

8 Now wait for it! If all goes well, your submarine will rise to the surface after a short time.

Why does it? You could do some experiments with the mixture of citric acid and soda bicarbonate to find out. (These things are not poisonous, but don't eat them!) Put some of the mixture into a glass of water and see what happens. Then I think you will know what makes the submarine rise. The reason is given in the usual place at the back of the book if you are still uncertain.

Finally, try making your model look still more like a submarine by covering up some of the gaps with some of mother's kitchen foil and putting some paint on.

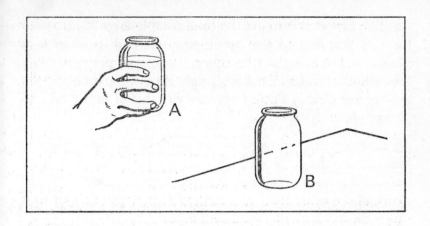

5 Making water flow uphill

It is surprising how much fun you can have with water. We all seem to like splashing around in it.

Water usually runs downhill, I think you will agree. Partly fill a jam-jar with water (A in the picture) and hold it up above another jam-jar (B in the picture) which is empty and standing on the kitchen table. Could you make the water go from jar A to jar B without tipping up the first jar? This would mean making the water go uphill over the edge of the first jar. It can be done if you use a thing called:

A Siphon

1 You need a piece of plastic tube, the kind that bends easily, about 1 metre long. Wash the tube out with warm water and washing-up liquid. Have jar A standing on something to be higher than B.

2 The first step is to get the tube completely filled up with water. You can do this by dipping one end in water in a bowl and sucking at the other. (You will perhaps get a mouthful of water! That is all right if both the tube and the water are clean.) Put a finger over each end of the tube to keep it full.

3 Keeping your fingers over the ends of the tube, put one end under the surface of the water in jar A. Let the other end hang down into jar B. Take your fingers away from the ends of the tube. If all goes well, the water will flow up and over the hill formed by the bent tube.

You can find out more about this siphon which you have made. Try to find the answers to these questions:

1 ` Will the water flow if there are air bubbles in the tube?
2 Will the water flow when the two jars are on the same level?
3 How can you make the water flow faster?

Can you think of places where the siphon is useful? I once saw a man who looked after boats on a river. He wanted to empty some water out of one of the boats. He did not have anyone to help him turn the boat upsidedown. Fortunately he had a short piece of rubber hose-pipe. With this he made a siphon.

Try to think of other times when a siphon would be used.

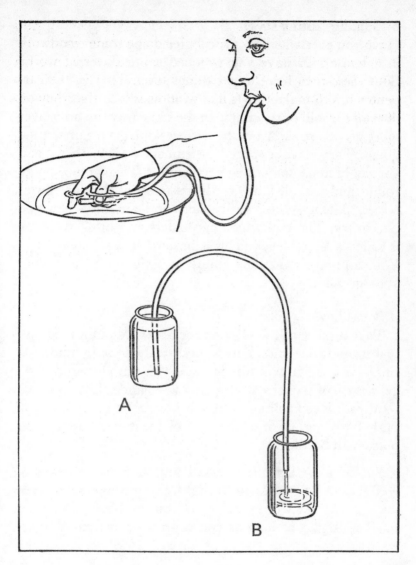

6 Getting things level

Have you ever watched a carpenter doing some woodwork in a house? Or have you watched a bricklayer at work? Both these men have to get things level. That is, the carpenter has to make things like window-sills so that they do not slope uphill or downhill. In the same way the bricklayer must get his rows of bricks neither sloping up nor sloping down. They have a special instrument to help them, and you could make something very similar. Then you could go round and test all kinds of things to see if they are level: tables, paving-stones, gas-cookers and anything else you like to try. The tool which carpenters and bricklayers use is called a 'spirit-level'. This is because it has alcohol in it. You can make something almost as useful with water in it. We can call it:

A Water-Level

1 Take a piece of the plastic tube about 205 mm long and seal it up at one end. This is most easily done by finding a small cork which will just fit in. If you cannot find a cork, get a strip of paper about 14 mm wide and roll it up into a tight roll. Keep rolling until you have a fat enough roll to push fairly tightly into the end of the tube. Fasten it in place with Bostik 1.

2 Put some water into a small jug. Add just a trace of washing-up liquid. Colour it slightly by putting one drop of ink in. (Mother will probably let you do this in one of her small milk jugs as long as you wash it out carefully afterwards.)

30

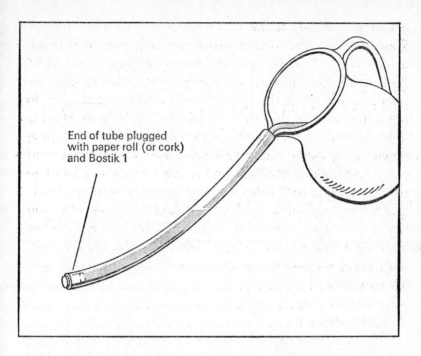

End of tube plugged
with paper roll (or cork)
and Bostik 1

3 Now pour some of this pale ink mixture into the open end of the plastic tube until it is about 20 mm from the top.

4 The next step is to seal the open end of the tube. You can do this with another cork, or else with another roll of paper and Bostik 1.

5 You now should have a length of plastic tube sealed at both ends with an air-bubble in the water. You will be able to make the air-bubble travel up and down the tube by tilting it. But the tube will bend easily and for a level tester we need something which will not bend.

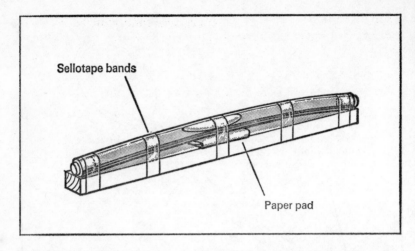

Sellotape bands

Paper pad

6 Take a piece of flat wood slightly longer than the tube. A ruler would do nicely. Fasten the plastic tube along the wood holding it in a few places with Sellotape. You will find it best to have a slight upward curve in the tube. You can get this by packing under the centre of the tube with a wad of paper. (See diagram.)

I think you will be able to decide for yourself how to use this 'water-level'. Try putting it on to things which are level and things which are sloping. You will soon find that the bubble in the tube always goes for the higher end. It will stay in the centre when the tube is level.

Why does the bubble go to the higher end? Why is it best to have the upward curve in the centre of the tube? These are some points for you to be thinking about as you go around testing the levels of things.

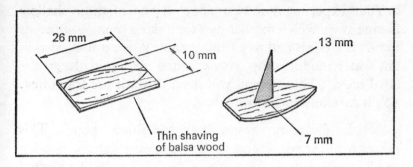

26 mm
10 mm
13 mm
7 mm
Thin shaving
of balsa wood

7 Experiments on a water surface

Strange things happen on water. If you try to float in the swimming-bath, you can only just about do it. But have you tried to *stand* on water? Some insects can stand on water all right. The surface of the water bends a bit, and then supports their weight. So, the surface of water can exert a force. This force can be changed by other liquids like oil and washing-up liquid. Very small light boats can be carried along by the surface force. Let us make some and call them:

Surface Boats

1 First make two little boats; very light ones. Cut each one from the thinnest possible piece of balsa wood (a shaving off a thicker piece will do). Cut each piece to a boat shape, as shown in the sketch, making it about 26 mm long and 10 mm across. Cut two sails out of a piece of post-card. Make them triangles, 13 mm tall and 7 mm at the base. Put a small blob of Bostik 1 on top of each piece of wood, set a sail in it, let it dry. There you have a light little boat.

2 Your experiment is best done in one of those shallow baking-trays which mother uses for baking sponges. It needs to be very clean and free from grease. Wash it in a bowl of hot water made frothy with washing-up liquid. Keep the bowl handy, because you will need to wash the tray often. Dry it carefully each time.

3 Put the clean tray where light can shine upon it. This means near the window or under an electric light. Use a cup to fill it with cold clean water. Can you see light reflected from the surface of the water? Perhaps you can see greasy streaks running across the surface too. If so, it is best to get rid of these by stroking the surface clean with absorbent kitchen or toilet paper.

4 Now sprinkle some pepper from a pepper-pot over the surface of the water. The aim of this is to help you see the surface and what is happening upon it. The lightest pieces of pepper stay on the surface. For a time the pepper will be swirling around showing the movement of the surface. Wait till the surface is still. Then put one drop of oil right in the centre. (The oil can be out of father's oil can, or it can be a drop of mother's cooking-oil taken out on the end of a milk straw.) If everything is nice and clean, you will see the oil spreading out over the surface in a perfect circle, pushing the pepper aside.

5 Now for the boats! Put them on the surface at one end of the tray, just about where the oil circle ends. Are they nice and still? Let's make them move! Put just one drop of washing-up liquid right at the end of the tray as shown in

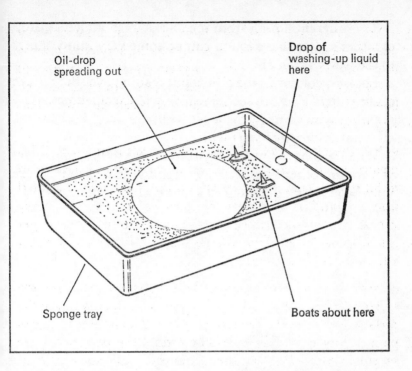

Oil-drop
spreading out

Drop of
washing-up liquid
here

Sponge tray

Boats about here

the drawing. It makes the surface of the water move and the boats go with it. Along they go, as if blown by a wind.

6 Do you want to make it all happen again? Take out the boats and stand them on a piece of paper to dry. Wash out the tray very carefully. Fill it with water and clean the surface if it looks greasy. Then it can all be done again. This time you may be able to get the boats into a better position so that they go further. Or you can have a game with a friend. Have one boat each and see whose goes furthest.

Try different liquids from the ones named above. A drop of father's after-shave lotion can do some very funny things to the water surface!

Look for colours in the oil-drop spreading over the surface of the water. You can see some lovely ones sometimes. Why is this do you think? It is a bit strange really, because the oil is not coloured to start with.

When you have finished trying all these things, make sure you wash mother's sponge tray carefully. If you don't, there may be a nasty oil-flavoured sponge when mother uses the tray next time!

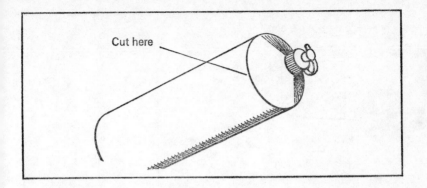

Cut here

8 Soaking experiments

Have you ever come home 'soaked through'? You know there are many materials like cloth which get soaked. Water can soak through them, and water can be soaked up by them. Both 'soaking through' and 'soaking up' are made use of in lots of things we do. Blotting paper is good for doing it. So are the paper coffee filters which your mother may use.

First try a 'soaking through' experiment in which you can get clean water from dirty water. This process is often called:

Filtering

1 Take an empty washing-up liquid bottle and cut right round at the point shown in the picture. Then cut a circle of blotting paper by folding a piece 102 mm square twice in half and cutting it as shown. Open it out to form a cone which will sit inside the top part of the bottle. Turned upsidedown this is rested on top of the bottom part of the bottle as you see in the picture on the next page.

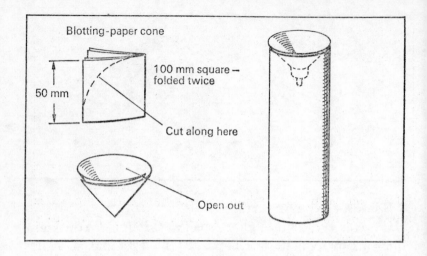

Blotting-paper cone

50 mm

100 mm square — folded twice

Cut along here

Open out

2 Can you find some muddy water in the garden? I am sure you can make some even if you cannot find it ready made! Pour it into the blotting-paper cone and wait. What comes through? What stays behind on the blotting-paper? By doing this once or twice you should begin to get nice clean water from muddy water. But do not drink it. Even if it looks clean enough to drink, there can still be bacteria in it which could be harmful.

Suppose you were in a desert and you *had* to drink water which you had cleared by filtering, how could you get rid of any bacteria?

Does this kind of filtering take colours out of water? Try it. Colour some water with a drop of ink, and then put it through your filter. Does the colour come through or stay behind?

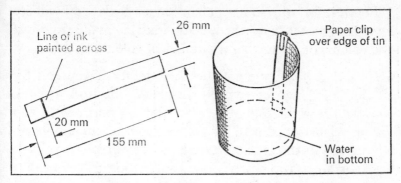

Line of ink painted across
26 mm
20 mm
155 mm
Paper clip over edge of tin
Water in bottom

Now let us try a 'soaking up' experiment. When it is done in laboratories with rather more expensive apparatus, this is called:

Chromatography

1 Cut some strips of blotting paper 26 mm wide and 155 mm long.

2 Choose a point upon one strip about 20 mm from one end. Use a small paint brush which you have dipped in ink to paint a line across the strip at this point. Leave it for a short time to dry.

3 Meanwhile you need to find a tin at least 155 mm tall. A carefully opened soup tin serves well for this. Put about 13 mm of water in the tin.

4 With a paper-clip at the top, hang the strip of blotting paper down the side of the tin inside, so that the bottom 13 mm is in the water. Your painted line of ink should be just above the water surface.

5 Leave it for 10 minutes. Then have a look. You will see something to tell you whether the ink was made from just one colour, or by mixing a number of colours together.

6 Now that you have got the basic method, you can try all kinds of things for yourself. Instead of ink from a bottle you can draw the line across the blotting paper with any colour of felt-tipped pen. Or you can use the colours which mother has in the kitchen for making coloured icing. Even blackcurrant syrup works. Try also putting a row of dots across a strip of blotting paper, instead of the line, making the dots different colours. This will give you a very pretty effect.

Be careful when you are doing this experiment not to get ink all over the place. Work on top of a few sheets of newspaper which will soak up any surplus ink.

Air Experiments

9 Air can make a thing go

Here is an exciting thing to make: one I made speeds across the carpet like the wind. I call it:

A Balloon-Powered Trolley

1 You need a piece of balsa wood about 100 mm long, 50 mm wide and 6 mm thick. Use Bostik 1 to stick two cocktail sticks across underneath to make axles.

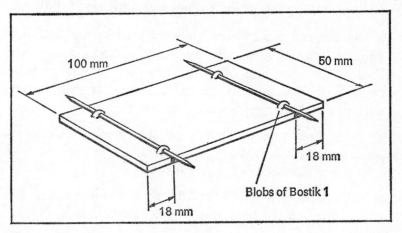

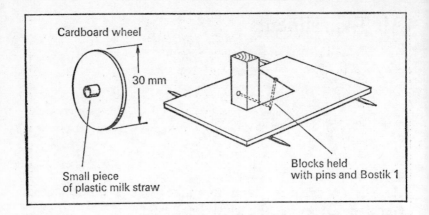

Cardboard wheel

30 mm

Small piece
of plastic milk straw

Blocks held
with pins and Bostik 1

2 Make wheels from four circles of fairly thick cardboard. Draw round an egg-cup to get the circles. Make holes in the centre of each and stick a little piece (6 mm) of drinking straw through each one.

3 Now fix two blocks (about 25 mm high), one straight and one sloping, on top of the trolley with pins and Bostik 1.

4 Get the red top from a bottle of washing-up liquid. If you are lucky mother will just have finished another one! Push it into one end of a 150 mm piece of plastic tube. Fix it with Sellotape to the block on top of your trolley, with one end sticking out over the back.

5 Now you are nearly ready. Put the wheels on the axles. Stick some extra little cardboard circles on the ends to stop the wheels from coming off.

6 Put a balloon over the red bottle top. Blow it up. Put your trolley on the floor and let go. WHOOSH! away it goes.

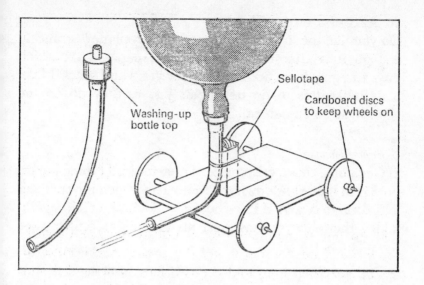

Washing-up bottle top

Sellotape

Cardboard discs to keep wheels on

You might like to make your trolley look more like a motor-car. This is easy by sticking thin cardboard round the sides and painting it. You can paint a driver to put inside too. And there is a lot more fun to have with this JET-POWERED trolley.

Why does it dash along? (Be careful. Don't say that the wind from the balloon blows it; that is blowing the wrong way!)

Some might say that it is like a rocket; can you see why?

Can you think of anything else it is like?

Could the same idea be used to make cars go on our roads?

You can see that there are many things to think about whilst you are having fun with this trolley.

10 Aeroplane test flights

Do you like the look of the Concorde aeroplane? Strangely enough it is almost the shape of the paper darts which boys and girls have been making for years and years. Make a dart like this to do test-flights just as they do on the 'Concorde'. You can call it:

A Paper 'Concorde'

1 Get a nice clean, crisp piece of quarto-sized typing paper. Fold it in half right down the middle and open it out. Then fold corners A and B into the centre fold. Now fold again, taking the folds you have just made into the centre. (See the pictures.)

2 The next step is to fold the two halves of the sheet together and lay it flat on the table. It should look like the third picture, with the single fold at the bottom and two folds at the top.

3 Two more folds to make, and your dart is finished. For the first of these, take the top fold X and bring it down to the bottom fold Y. Turn over and do the same on the other side.

4 Press the folds well down. Then open them out to give the dart shown. It will tend to open up in the middle. Put in a few drops of Bostik 1, or use some Sellotape to stop this.

5 The time has come for the first test-flight. Make sure the dart is nice and straight. Hold it between finger and thumb at about the point P. Hold it well up in the air, and

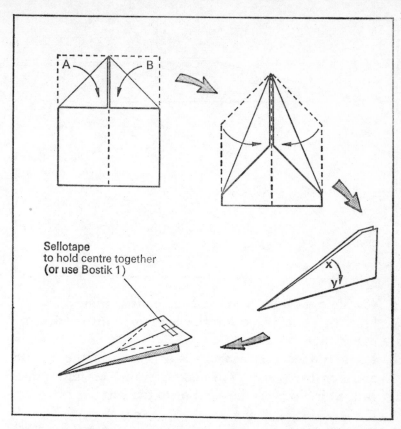

Sellotape
to hold centre together
(or use Bostik 1)

launch it with a nice steady throw. Away it should go upon a good steady glide.

6 Each time you do a test-flight, first of all make sure that the nose of your 'Concorde' is straight. Smooth it out between your fingers. Each time it lands it gets crumpled up. It is a good thing it does not happen to the real Concorde!

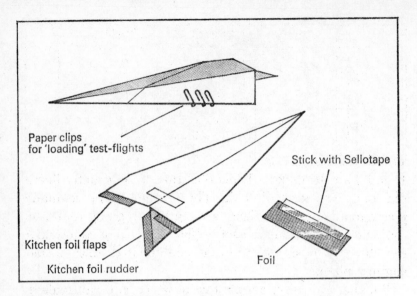

Paper clips
for 'loading' test-flights

Stick with Sellotape

Kitchen foil flaps

Kitchen foil rudder

Foil

7 Now do test-flights to try out some other things:

a. Find the best place for the load to be carried using paper clips.

b. Fix a rudder and wing flaps as shown in the picture and find the best way of making your 'Concorde' turn in the air either to the right or to the left.

You will find that it is not easy to control a plane. It is most important to have the load in the right place. For turning, it is not just a matter of turning the rudder as it is on a ship. Some of the things which I found out with the 'paper Concorde' are in the usual place at the back of the book. Have a look on page 86 and see if you have found the same things.

46

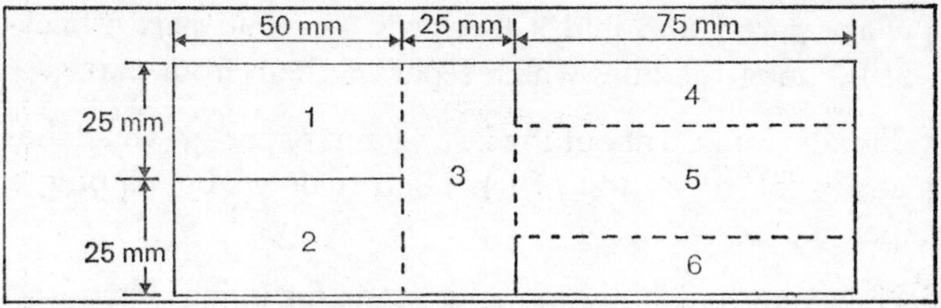

The diagram shows a rectangle divided into sections with the following measurements along the top: 50 mm, 25 mm, 75 mm. Along the left side: 25 mm, 25 mm. The sections are numbered 1, 2 (left), 3 (middle), 4, 5, 6 (right).

11 Helicopter trials

If you want to make a helicopter that looks exactly like a real one, it is very difficult. There seem to be so many pieces to a helicopter. There are big blades going round on top, and there is a smaller set of blades spinning round near the tail. It looks much more complicated than a jet-engined plane.

But there is a very simple model which you can make if you just want something which spins round in the air. Let's call it:

A Paper Whirler

1 Take a piece of fairly stiff white paper 50 mm wide and 150 mm long.

2 Draw lines in pencil upon the paper to divide it into six parts using the measurements shown. You will see that the parts are numbered from 1 to 6. Some lines are shown full and heavy, some are just dotted.

3 With a pair of scissors, cut along the heavy lines. Now fold along the dotted line between 4 and 5, so that 4 goes in towards the centre. Do the same with part 6.

4 Take part 1 and fold it forwards, and fold part 2 backwards, along the lines which separate them from part 3.

5 Finally, fold up about the last 13 mm of part 5 (which has 4 and 6 folded on top of it). Hold it down by slipping a paper clip across it.

6 Now your helicopter model is ready for flying. Hold it as high as you can and let it drop. Does it spin as it falls? How could you make it spin the other way? If you have an idea, try it out and see if it works.

What other things can you do with this model? You can make it look very attractive as it falls by painting one side in one colour and the other side completely different. Or you can make two helicopters and let them fall both at once side by side. It is fun to have them going round in opposite directions as they are falling. If you have a number of friends joining in the game, you can have six or eight of them all landing together in the same area.

There are some trees that have seeds with the same kind of helicopter wings as your model. Do you know the names of some? Why are the seeds like this? We certainly cannot accuse the trees of imitating helicopters; they started doing it first.

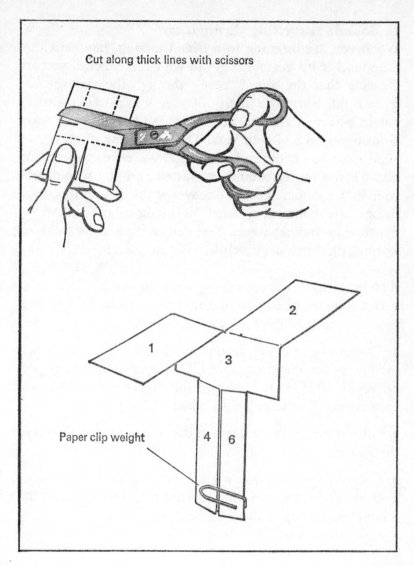

Cut along thick lines with scissors

Paper clip weight

49

12 Sounds travelling through air

When you are listening to a friend talking, how is it that the sound of his voice can get to your ears? Yes, if you are thinking that the sound travels through the air, you are quite right. From the mouth of your friend sound spreads out in waves in all directions. A small part of each wave lands upon each of your ears. Then you hear.

Suppose you could stop the sound waves from spreading out. Then a lot less would be wasted and you would hear your friend louder. People discovered this a long time ago. Before telephones they used 'speaking-tubes' to talk to someone in another room. You can easily make something working on the same principle. We can call it:

A Hearing Tube

1 Get a metre of flexible plastic tube. It can be longer if you want to hear over a bigger distance.

2 Then you need two plastic funnels. The little ones which mother uses in the kitchen for filling things like pepper-pots do very well. Or you can use the bigger ones which are used for pouring liquids into bottles.

3 Put one funnel in each end of the plastic tube as shown in the picture.

4 You will find that you have something now to help you hear very faint sounds. Put one funnel to your ear and the other close to any of these things:

A watch or a clock.

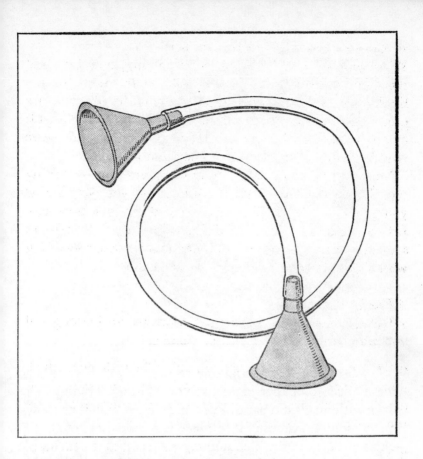

A radio set with the volume turned down.

A pin being scratched on paper.

In each case you will hear the sound much louder. You can also, of course, get a friend to speak into the other end, or you can use your 'hearing tube' as a doctor uses a stethoscope.

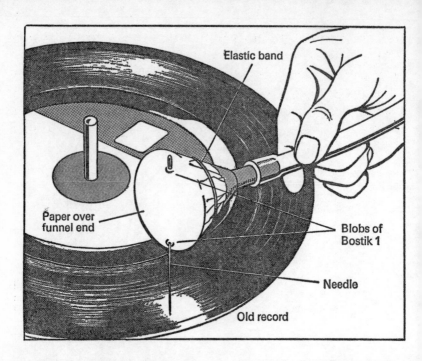

Elastic band

Paper over funnel end

Blobs of Bostik 1

Needle

Old record

5 Try listening to gramophone records in a different way. Put a piece of paper right over one funnel, holding it in place with an elastic band. Put a needle through it as shown in the picture, fastening it in place with two blobs of Bostik. 1. Put an *old* record which nobody wants on to the turntable of a record-player. Switch on so that the record goes round, but do not put on the normal needle arm. Hold the needle of your 'hearing tube' in the record groove putting the other funnel to your ear. Then you will hear sounds and music very much like people did when the gramophone was first invented. Where do the sounds come from?

There are many other sounds you will want to try your 'hearing tube' out on. To do a bigger experiment, you can try using the long plastic hose which father uses for watering the garden. Try it one day when he has got it out, making sure it is empty of water. You will not need funnels because it is wider tubing, but you may have to ask father to take the nozzle off.

Balance Experiments

13 Balancing coins

There was a time in England when real gold coins were in common use. Then it was possible for small pieces of gold to be clipped off the coins before spending them. This gave the dishonest 'clippers' a profit and the coins got smaller. It is not worthwhile for anybody to clip pieces off our coins today. Even so, it is quite interesting to check the weights of our 2p, 1p, and ½p coins. From balsa wood you can make a simple:

Coin Balance

1 With Bostik 1 stick two lengths of 6 mm square balsa wood strip together side by side to form a beam 12 mm wide and 280 mm long.

2 With a pencil draw a line across the centre of the top face of the beam. Put a 1p piece carefully over this line so that it comes equally either side. Draw a line around as much of it as you can. Take away the 1p and you will have two curved lines as shown in the second diagram. Label them 'o' and 'o'.

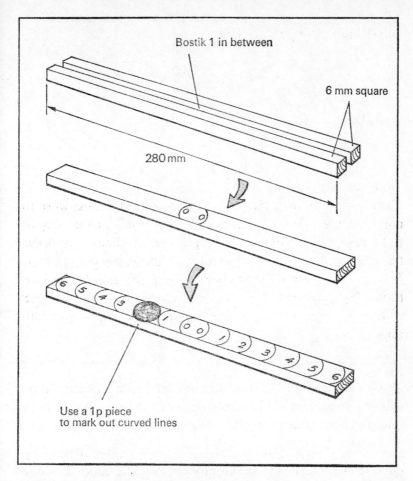

Bostik 1 in between

6 mm square

280 mm

Use a 1p piece
to mark out curved lines

3 Draw other curved lines as shown, spaced by just the width of a 1p piece, on both sides of the beam. Label them 1, 2, 3, etc. up to 6. Cut off whatever is left of the beam at each end.

55

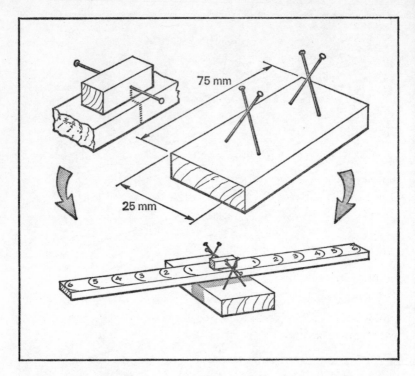

4 Cut a small length of 6 mm square balsa strip making it 18 mm long. Stick it in the middle of the beam between the two 'o' lines. Put pins exactly in the middle of each side of it (see the picture).

5 Use crossed pins to make supports for the beam as shown in the next picture. Try your beam on the supports for balance. If it does not rest horizontal put a drawing pin stuck in underneath on the lighter side, moving it up and down until the balance is right.

6 Now you can test coins. Put a 1p piece on each side of the centre with its outer edge just touching the '3' line. If they are equal in weight, the beam should balance. If it does not, is it the older looking one which seems lighter? Try a number of different 1p pieces. You will find some differences, I think, but the differences in weight will not be large.

7 Try putting a pile of two 1p pieces against the line marked '2' on one side of your balance beam. Can you balance this with a single 1p piece on the other side? It will not go by the line marked '2'. Where does it need to go? (This is like a see-saw with a fat child on one side and a thin child on the other!)

8 Now try three 1p pieces in a pile against the line marked '2' on one side. Can these be balanced by a single 1p piece? Try to guess where it ought to go first, then see if your guess is right.

There are all kinds of other tests which you can do with your 'coin balance'. For example, is a 10p piece ten times as heavy as a 1p piece? Try out as many tests as you can think of.

14 Balancing toys

Take a nice long pencil and balance it upright upon the tip of your nose. You can't? Well, yes, it *is* a bit difficult to do normally. Nevertheless, here is a way to make:

The Balancing Pencil

1 Use a long pencil well sharpened. The kind which has six sides is easier to use than a round one. You also need two plastic milk straws. About 25 mm up from the sharpened end of the pencil, strap one milk straw to a flat side of the pencil using Sellotape. Fasten it as shown in the picture so that most of the straw sticks out beyond the end of the pencil point. Now fasten the other milk straw in just the same way on the exactly opposite side of the pencil.

2 The next step is to make the milk straws stand away from the pencil. To do this, put a pin through one straw a little below the Sellotape towards the pencil point. Push it into the sharpened part of the pencil. Pull the milk straw outwards, and put a small piece of Sellotape on the milk straw to cover up the pin's head. Do the same with the other straw.

3 Now you are nearly ready for your balancing act. Use Sellotape again to fasten a new penny to the bottom end of each milk straw. Now, put the pencil point on the tip of one finger and you will find it will balance there. Having gained confidence, try it on the tip of your nose. Yes! You can do it!

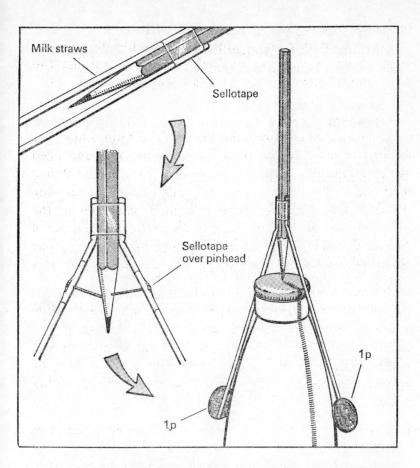

Milk straws

Sellotape

Sellotape over pinhead

1p

1p

It is also fun to balance the pencil point on something like the top of a full bottle of milk before it is opened. (Do not push the pencil point *through* the bottle top: it will rest on top all right.) Give it a twirl, and it spins round and round.

Why does the pencil balance so well like this? There is something here for you to discover. And the same sort of method can be used to make:

A Balancing Man

1 Draw the shape of a man on a postcard. Give him long legs fairly wide apart. Measure 18 mm down from where his legs join and draw a line across as shown. Now with a pair of scissors cut the man out.

2 Next you have to make a pulley wheel. Do this from a slice cut off a bottle cork stuck in between two circles of card. Make the circles by drawing round a 10p piece. Push a wooden cocktail stick through the centre after making a hole right through first of all with a big pin.

3 Cut a piece of plastic milk straw just as long as the distance from A to B on the man's legs. Stick it right across both legs, on the line A to B using Bostik 1 in blobs. When quite dry, use scissors to cut a gap in the middle of the milk straw just a little wider than the pulley wheel which you have made. Then fit the pulley in as shown. Stick 1p coins to the man's feet with Sellotape.

4 Now you will find that your man will balance on his wheel upon a horizontal piece of string. It is much the same as the balancing pencil. Make the string slope and the man runs along it. It looks almost as though he is walking the tight-rope.

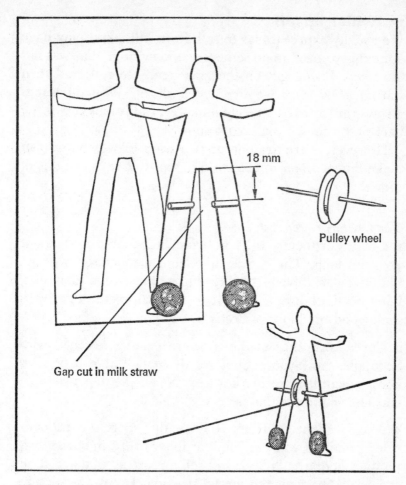

18 mm

Pulley wheel

Gap cut in milk straw

Have you discovered why these things balance yet? See if you agree with the reasons given on pages 87 and 88.

15 Rolling up hill

We usually expect things to roll down hills. You may have done this yourself upon some nice grassy slope that was not too steep. If you got on the grass ready to roll, and then started *uphill*, you would have a shock. Why do things always roll down? I expect you know, but it tells you at the back of the book if you do not know.

However, there are one or two ways in which you can make things *appear* to behave differently. Let us call one of these:

The Contrary Cardboard Tube

1 Get a cardboard tube as wide as possible and about 100 mm long. The centre tube from a toilet roll will do, but a wider tube is better. Put a nail inside the tube, lying on the bottom. Stick it to the wall of the tube with some good big blobs of Bostik 1.

2 Cover both ends of the tube with paper fastened with Sellotape. Now you cannot see the nail. But you need to know where it is, so mark a tiny 'X' on the paper at each end just where the nail is.

3 Make a slight hill from a book with a sheet of cardboard resting on it. If you put your cardboard tube in one special position upon the 'hill', it will roll up instead of down. You can probably guess the special position. If not, the picture shows you where the 'X' should be. It will not roll far uphill, of course. It is quite a surprise to see it start in the 'wrong' direction.

62

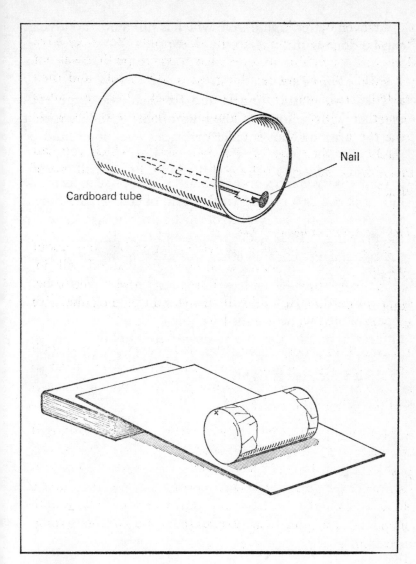

Nail

Cardboard tube

An even better 'uphill' roll, which is still more mystifying, can be done with:

The Wandering Funnels

1 Take two plastic funnels and fix their two large ends together with Sellotape. The ones about 75 mm across at the top are best, but smaller or bigger ones could also be used.

2 Now cut two pieces of cardboard of equal size to form the hill. It is rather a special kind of hill, of course, and only a slight one. Make each piece of cardboard the size shown in the drawing, a little wider at one end than the other. Join the two narrow ends together with a hinge made of Sellotape.

3 Your cardboard 'hill' will now stand up on its own if you separate the two wide ends by about 35 mm. Put the taped funnels upon it. Yes, they slowly roll uphill! Can you explain why? You probably can. Look in the usual place to see if your idea is right.

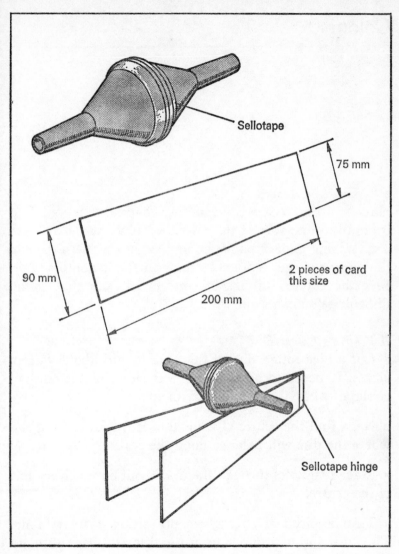

Sellotape

75 mm

90 mm

200 mm

2 pieces of card this size

Sellotape hinge

Colours

16 Mixing colours

Have you ever heard someone say that white is made up
from all the colours of the rainbow? If so, you may have
tried mixing a lot of paints hoping to get white. In the end
that way you get a horrid mess. So try it another way.
Mix the colours up inside your eyes. Does that sound
difficult? You can do it with:

A Whirling Colour Disc

1 Cut a nice round disc of thick cardboard about 75 mm
across. It needs to be white on both sides. If it is not, cut
circles of white paper and stick them on.

2 Next, find the centre of your disc. How? By finding just
where the disc will balance upon the point of a needle.

3 Make two holes through the disc about 6 mm either side
of the centre.

4 Take a piece of strong, smooth string 1 metre long.
Thread it through one hole in the disc and back through

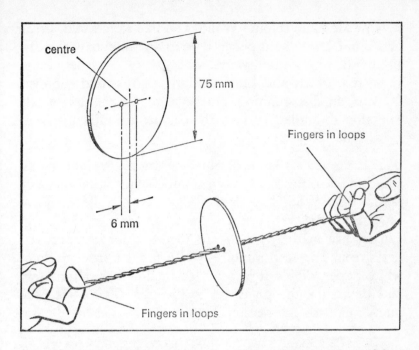

centre

75 mm

6 mm

Fingers in loops

Fingers in loops

the other hole. Tie the two ends of the string together with a knot which will not slip.

5 No colours yet, but have a trial spin. Get the disc in the centre of the strong loop with two or three fingers of each hand through the ends. Swing the disc round in the centre like turning a skipping rope, with the string a bit slack. Pull your hands apart to tighten the string suddenly, and the disc should start spinning. Pull again as it comes to rest. It should start spinning the other way. As long as you keep pulling and slackening, it should keep spinning, first one way and then the other way.

6 Now for some colour! Would you like to mix red, green and blue? Draw faint pencil lines upon one side of the disc to divide it up into twelve wedge-shaped pieces. Paint these red, green and blue, working right round the disc. Now set the disc spinning. Your eyes get the colours quickly one after the other. In fact, the colours are mixed in your eyes. What do you see?

7 You can try all kinds of other mixtures. Try putting all the colours of the rainbow in small wedges upon one side of the disc. What are they? Red, orange, yellow, green, blue and violet. What do you get when these mix? Or you can try just mixing two colours together, for instance, red and green. For each mixture, you just cut a fresh circle of white paper, divide it into wedges, paint them alternately and then stick the paper on to the disc. There are very many mixtures you can make.

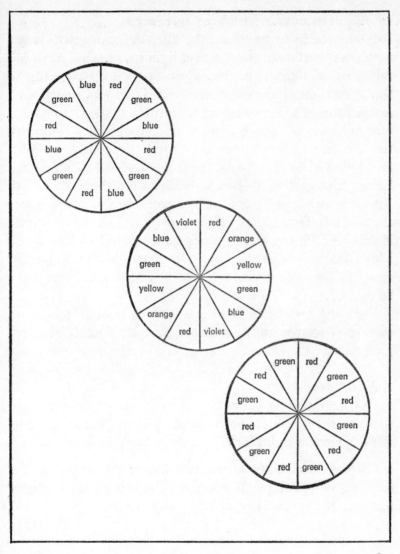

17 Experiments with shiny surfaces

It is interesting to go round the kitchen looking for things with shiny surfaces. These reflect light in a special way. All things reflect light, of course. That is how it is we see them. But some things reflect light *regularly*. Then we can actually see pictures of other things in their surfaces. A mirror is the best example of this. But there are many other things in the kitchen which reflect clear pictures. Try looking at your face reflected in saucepans, the fronts and backs of spoons, knives, plates, cups, glasses, stainless steel dishes, and so on. Try as many shiny things as you can find in fact. In some things your face will look its right size. In other things it will look bigger, and in other things it will look smaller. Make a note of where you see your face right size, bigger or smaller. Then see if you agree with what is given on pages 88 and 89.

Even the surface of Sellotape is shiny enough to give a picture. You can use it to reflect light and make coloured patterns in:

A Kaleidoscope

1 Cut three oblong pieces of stiff cardboard, two long ones and one short one as shown in the picture. Paint one side of each piece a dull black.

2 On the black sides of the two longer pieces put a flat covering of Sellotape. If you use 25 mm wide tape, it will just fit right across. Try to avoid any creases.

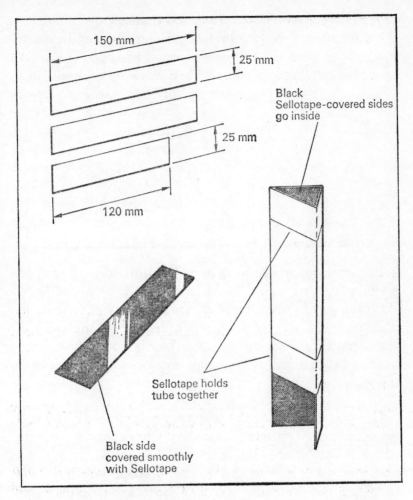

150 mm

25 mm

25 mm

120 mm

Black
Sellotape-covered sides
go inside

Sellotape holds
tube together

Black side
covered smoothly
with Sellotape

3 Now bind the three pieces of card together with Sellotape to form a kind of three-sided tube, with a gap in one side at the bottom. This makes your kaleidoscope.

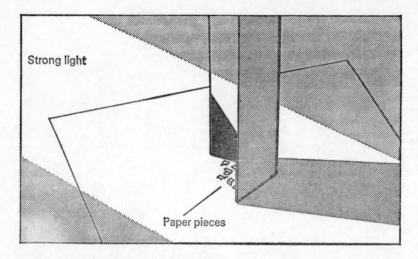

Strong light

Paper pieces

4 Put some coloured pieces of paper, little torn-up bits, on a white sheet of paper. Make sure there is plenty of light. With the gap in the tube at the bottom, towards the light, look down the tube at the pieces of paper. I think you will see a pattern. How many sides has it got? Move your tube and the pattern will change. Try looking at all kinds of things.

Can you decide how the patterns are produced? You will get much better patterns of course if you can use something which reflects more clearly than Sellotape. See if you can find something else to use. A kaleidoscope you buy in a shop has two mirrors instead of Sellotape-covered card. If you can find two small mirrors, try them out and you will get clearer patterns. There are all kinds of things which you can try.

Magnets and Electricity

18 Experiments with magnets

Men have been fascinated by magnets all through the ages. At first they used pieces of rock found already magnetized in the earth. Such a rock was called a 'lodestone'. Sometimes good specimens were mounted in rich and costly settings. Rich men had them to interest their friends.

You can do your own experiments these days, not with a 'lodestone', but with a strong little 'Eclipse' magnet bought in an ironmonger's shop. Get the horseshoe kind. When you get it there will be a piece of iron called a 'keeper' across its ends. Take this off for experiments. Put it back when you have finished. This helps the magnet to 'keep' its magnetism.

Now try some work on:

Sticking to Magnets

1 What will a magnet pick up? Try nails, paper-fasteners, pins, paper, wood, drawing-pins, pennies, ten-penny pieces, glass, and so on. Try all kinds of things. Put all the things which stick to the magnet in one pile. Is there anything about all these which is the same? This is not an

easy question, but see if you can spot the answer. Then see if you agree with the answer at the end of the book.

2 Does this strange force of a magnet pass through things like paper and cardboard? Try it and see. Use some nails or pins which you have already found to be the kind which stick to the magnet. Sprinkle them on a piece of cardboard and move the magnet underneath. Does the magnetic force go through the card?

Now try making up a magnet trick. A friend of mine calls it:

Mahatma

1 Mount the horseshoe magnet in the tray part of a matchbox using plasticine or Bostik 1 to hold it close to one end as shown. The keeper will then stick to the outside end of the tray.

2 Use Sellotape to fasten four plastic milk straws to the tray to form four legs. Then force the outside part of the matchbox over them. This gives you the whole matchbox ready to stand on four milk straw legs with the magnet hidden inside.

3 Make a base for this to stand on out of a piece of cardboard or balsa wood about 125 mm long and 75 mm wide. In the centre of this base make four holes, A, B, C and D, to take four small pegs made out of pieces of cocktail stick about 12 mm long. Stick these in with Bostik 1. Right in the centre of the base also make a very fine hole with a needle,

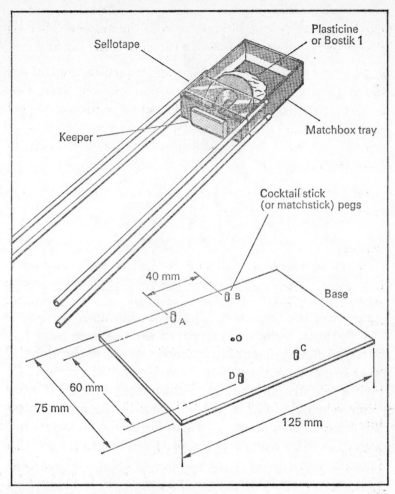

Sellotape

Plasticine
or Bostik 1

Keeper

Matchbox tray

Cocktail stick
(or matchstick) pegs

40 mm

B

Base

A

O

C

D

60 mm

75 mm

125 mm

('o' in the picture). Use the needle to thread a piece of
cotton through the hole and fix it.

4 The time has come to mount the matchbox. The four

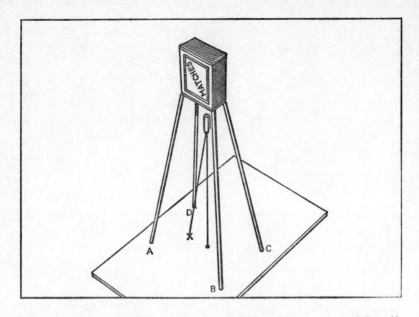

legs go over the pegs A, B, C, and D with a spot of Bostik
1 to fix them. Take the keeper off the box now, and put
the paper clip in place of it. Thread the cotton through the
paper clip and gently pull on the free end of the cotton 'X'.
It will gradually pull the clip off the box, and then will come
a time when the clip is just hovering in the air, with no
visible means of support. You can fasten the cotton with a
touch of Bostik 1 when it is just the right length for the clip
to hover.

To anyone not knowing the magnet is inside the match-
box, this looks like magic. It looks like the 'Indian Rope
Trick'. That is why my friend calls it an Indian name like
'Mahatma'.

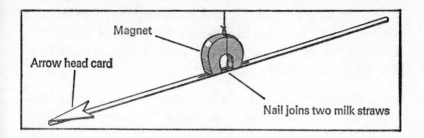

Magnet

Arrow head card

Nail joins two milk straws

19 A magnet as a direction finder

One of the first things that men found about the magnetic pieces of rock was that they could be used for showing the way on land and on sea. This is the reason for the name 'lodestone'. It means 'leading-stone'.

You can use your magnet in the same way to make:

A Magnetic Compass

1 First make a direction pointer from two milk straws. Join them together by means of an oval-headed 50 mm nail. The head of the nail will push fairly tightly into one end of one milk straw; the other end of the nail will go more loosely into the other milk straw. Stick an arrowhead piece of thin card to one end of the two joined straws, and you have your pointer.

2 Now take a piece of cotton, the thinnest you can find. It needs to be about a metre long. Tie loops at both ends. Slip the magnet through one loop. Then you will find that you can fasten the pointer to the magnet very simply. Just hold the magnet over the join of the two milk straws where the nail is. Up it jumps and is fixed.

3 Slip the loop at the other end of the cotton over a wooden stick or ruler. Rest the stick across the backs of two chairs, as shown. Your magnet with its pointer should then hang just a few centimetres clear of the floor.

4 What does it do first of all? It twists round and round. Why? Leave it for about a quarter of an hour. It will then have come to rest. Find out if it always comes to rest in the same direction. To do this, put a piece of wood on the floor close to the arrowhead where it first comes to rest. Twist the magnet and pointer into some other direction. Leave it again. Come back to see if the arrowhead is once again by the block of wood. Try it as often as you like. It is very likely that you will always find it settled in the same direction.

5 Ask somebody, perhaps your father (he knows lots of things), which way is North and South. For a compass it is best to have the arrow pointing North. As you have set it up, yours may point South. But it is easy to put it right. Just turn the pointer round on the magnet.

Now you have made yourself a rather big and cumbersome compass. But it would nevertheless help you to find your way. Mountaineers and explorers carry much smaller compasses. Try to get a look at one. Does it look as if there is a magnet in it? What is there instead of a piece of cotton? It is certainly much more convenient than the one you made, but the principle is just the same.

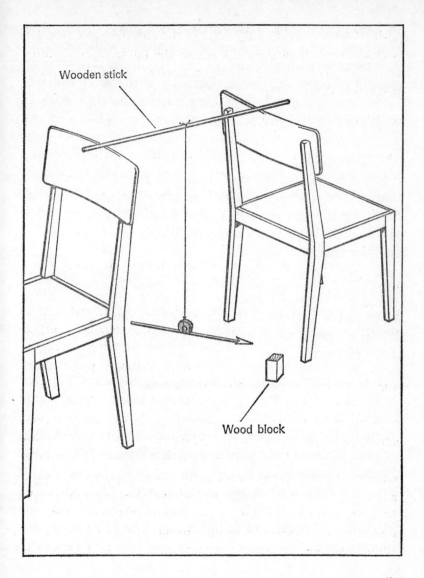

Wooden stick

Wood block

20 An experiment with static electricity

You have been doing some experiments with magnets; try one now with electricity. The two have always been thought of together. Static electricity is the kind which is made usually by rubbing things. Lightning is the same kind. We can call this experiment:

The Dancing Scraps

1 You need a shallow tin. It can be round or square or oblong. 100 mm across is about the right size. The best depth for it is 25 mm. A tuna fish tin opened smoothly will do well. Wash it out thoroughly, and you can get rid of the fishy smell!

2 The first step is to put in a 'dancing floor'. If the tin is just 25 mm deep, all that needs to be done is to stick white paper to the bottom of the tin inside. If the tin is deeper, you will have to raise the floor up off the bottom as shown in the picture.

3 Now put in the scraps which are going to dance. You can be a real experimenter here and try all kinds of light small things. I have tried:

Small pieces of paper, 12 mm square, loosely crumpled.
Small pieces of crumpled aluminium kitchen foil.
Seeds of various kinds.
Small scraps of cloth and pieces of wool.
Small pieces of plastic.

You can try all kinds of things, which you just put on the 'dancing floor'.

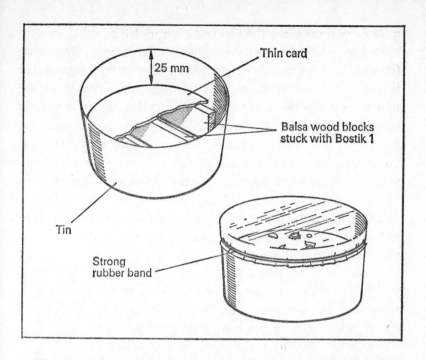

25 mm

Thin card

Balsa wood blocks
stuck with Bostik 1

Tin

Strong
rubber band

4 Finally you cover the tin with the material which you
are going to rub to produce the static electricity. You can
experiment with this again, using all kinds of transparent
plastic sheet materials. As a start, try an empty plastic bag
of the kind which mother buys paper serviettes in. Or try
the transparent cooking foil which comes in rolls for baking.
Or try the transparent envelope which you buy a birthday
card in. Use two sheets of the material, big enough to
cover the mouth of the tin. Stretch the double thickness
across the top as tightly as you can, putting a strong
elastic band round to hold it in place.

5 Now you produce the electric charges by rubbing briskly over the plastic. Sometimes you can do it with your bare fingers. At other times, rubbing with a woollen fluffy duster is best. You have to be patient. Usually there comes a time when up jump the scraps and stick to the plastic cover. It reminds you of the way pieces of iron jump up to stick to a magnet. Then you can make the scraps dance by bringing your finger near to them. Often they will scamper away and you can chase them round with the tip of your finger.

This experiment works better some days than others. Do not be disappointed if you strike a bad day. Try it again when the sun is shining.

Where else do you come across static electricity? Have you heard tiny crackles as you take off nylon clothes? In the dark you can sometimes see tiny flashes of light. This is clearly electricity. How has it been produced?

Answers to Questions

1 Hero's Handkerchief Experiment
Why does the handkerchief not get wet?
Because air is trapped in the glass tumbler. As long as it is there, water cannot get in.

Water that does not fall
Why does the water stay in the glass?
Because air under the card pushes upwards with a force which is greater than the weight of the water which is trying to push the card down.

2 The Magic Can
Why does water not run out of the bottom hole unless the top one is uncovered?
Because air must get *in* if water is to come *out*.

3 The Obedient Diver
How can you make the diver go down?
Just *squeeze* the sides of the plastic bottle.

Why does it make him go down?

Squeezing the bottle increases the pressure everywhere inside. This makes *more* water go into the tube fastened to the back of the diver. You will have found already that *more* water in the diver's tube makes him sink.

4 The Lolly Stick Submarine

What makes the submarine come up?

I expect you found that when the citric acid and the soda bicarbonate are put into water together, bubbles start coming from the mixture. These are bubbles of carbon dioxide. In your submarine, the bubbles collect in the conning-tower. This makes the submarine more buoyant and up it comes.

5 A Siphon

Will water flow if there are air-bubbles in the tube?

I found that it *would* flow if there are just a few small bubbles. But, if a lot of the tube is full of air, the water will *not* flow.

Will the water flow when the two jars are on the same level?

No, this is when the flow stops.

How can you make the water flow faster?

Water flows faster if you make a bigger difference in height between the two jars.

Other uses of a siphon:

To empty water out of a garden pond which needs cleaning.
To empty an aquarium tank without lifting it.

To transfer wine from a large jar to a bottle.
Perhaps you thought of some others too.

6 A 'Water'-Level
Why does the water go to the higher end?
Because air is 'lighter' than water.
Why is it best to have an upward curve in the tube?
You will find that if you have the tube flat, you cannot
get the bubble to stay still. The slight upward curve helps
it a little to come to rest in the centre.

7 Surface Boats
Why do you see colours in the spreading oil drop?
You know that white light is made of a mixture of all the
colours of the rainbow. Because of its extreme thinness, the
oil layer cannot reflect *all* of these. You see a mixture of
the ones it *can* reflect. This is usually an attractive colour.

8 Filtering
How could you get rid of bacteria from water?
(You know what bacteria are, don't you? Another word
for them is 'germs'. They are very small living things.
Some of them cause diseases.) Since the bacteria are alive,
you can get rid of them by boiling the water. This kills
them, so they can do no harm.
Does filtering take colours out of water?
Not usually.

Chromatography

You will find that as mixtures of colours soak up on the blotting paper, some colours go further than others. This means that you can see some of the various colours which have been put into the ink or other liquid. For example, I found that my 'permanent black ink' was made from a mixture of blue, black, yellow and green.

9 A Balloon-Powered Trolley

Why does the trolley dash along?

Because air is being forced *backwards* out of the balloon. To balance this, if the trolley is free to move, it *has* to go *forwards*. (Try throwing a heavy ball to a friend when you are standing on skates!)

Why is it like a rocket?

Because a rocket does the same kind of thing. It throws flames and hot gases backwards.

What other things is it like?

It is like a hose-pipe from which water is flowing fast. (Firemen find their hoses hard to hold.)

It is like an aeroplane jet-engine.

Can the same idea be used to drive motor-cars?

Yes, if the cars are well spaced out!

10 A Paper 'Concorde'

What is the best place for the 'load' of paper clips?

I found this to be about half-way along.

How do you make the plane turn?

I found that if you want to make a turn to the right, then

the rudder must be turned *right*, the left hand flap must be *up* and the right hand flap *down*.

11 A Paper Whirler
How do you make it spin the other way?
Reverse the blades 1 and 2.
What are the names of trees with seeds which whirl like this?
There are two common ones: sycamore and ash.

12 A Hearing Tube
Where do the sounds on a record come from?
In the grooves of the record very small irregularities have been produced which match the sound to be heard. The needle which you use hits against these as the record goes round.

13 Coin Balance
Where does a single 1p piece on one side have to be placed to balance two 1p pieces on the other side against the line marked '2'?
It has to be against the line marked '4'.
Where does a single 1p piece on one side have to be placed to balance three 1p pieces on the other side against the line marked '2'?
It has to be against the line marked '6'.
Is a 10p piece ten times as heavy as a 1p piece?
No, I found it between three and four times as heavy.

14 The Balancing Pencil
Why does the pencil balance?
Because the pennies on the milk straws bring *most* of the

weight below the point of the pencil, which is the point at which the weight is supported.

A Balancing Man

Why does the man balance on the string?
In this case too, the pennies make *most* of the weight come below the wheel upon which the man is supported.

15 The Wandering Funnels

Why do the funnels appear to roll up hill?
If you look carefully you will see that they are really sinking *lower* as they roll.

16 A Whirling Colour Disc

What colour do you see when red, green and blue are mixed?
The colours disappear to give grey.
What do you see when the colours of the rainbow are mixed?
This time you get a paler grey. (If you could get paints *exactly* like rainbow colours, you would get white.)
What do you see with red and green mixed?
A kind of yellow.

17 Shiny Surfaces

What do you look like reflected in:
The shiny outsides of saucepans, etc?
Tall and thin.
The backs of spoons?
Smaller in all directions.

The insides of spoons?
Smaller and upsidedown! (but bigger and right way up when very close).

A Kaleidoscope
How many sides has the pattern got?
I think you will see six.
How are the patterns produced?
The reflection of anything in one Sellotape 'mirror' gets reflected a second time in the other 'mirror'.

18 Sticking to Magnets
Does the magnetic force go through card?
Yes, I am sure you will find that it does.

19 A Magnetic Compass
Why does the magnet twist round and round at first?
Because the cotton is made up of twisted strands which tend to unwind.
Can you see the magnet in a mountaineer's compass?
Yes, in many of them, the pointed needle is itself a magnet.
What is there in a mountaineer's compass instead of cotton?
The magnet swings upon a pointed pin.

20 Static Electricity
How are the sparks made with nylon clothes?
They are produced by the rubbing which goes on all day long when you are wearing them.

In the same series

Ask me a question

by J. Perry Harvey

All knowledge is exciting and it is quite remarkable how much you can learn without even thinking about it. You can have a lot of fun, too, from the many and varied quizzes which make up *Ask me a question*. They lead on to all kinds of interesting points of discovery and, at the same time, provide hours of amusement.

The Zebra Cookbook

by Maureen Williams

A first cookery book full of ideas for simple meals and snacks.

Do you like craftwork?

The Zebra Book of Papercraft

by G. Roland Smith

A hundred different models, all made with paper and without a knife; they all take very little time and can often be joined together if you want to build up a really impressive construction.

Models from Junk

Junk on the Move

by Brenda B. Jackson

With the help of the simple instructions in these books many models and creatures can be created out of the bits and pieces to be found in every home.

Books of hobbies

The Zebra Indoor Book

by Rita Davies

Filled with an abundance of ideas for things to collect and make.

The Zebra Outdoor Book

by Frederick Wilkinson

Full of ideas that will start an absorbing hobby or fill a free afternoon.

Make your own Collection

by Joyce and Cyril Parsons

All kinds of suggestions for preparing, arranging, displaying and adding to specimens so that an accumulation of objects becomes a real collection.

Reference books

The Zebra Book of Facts for Girls

The Zebra Book of Facts for Boys

compiled by Cyril and Joyce Parsons

These books contain all kinds of facts about World History and Geography, Science and Mathematics, National and Local Government. For enthusiasts there are sporting records, nature notes, codes and ciphers and First Aid information. There is a special section for cyclists and a number of suggestions for things to do on a wet day or on a long journey. They are, in fact, packed with fascinating information which boys and girls will find most useful.

The Zebra Dictionary in Colour

compiled by Leonard Wise

This Zebra Special has full-colour photographs on every page, and the attractive layout and clear definitions make this new reference book easy to use and give it a special appeal for a wide range of young people.